# One Last Card Trick

A comedy

## Stewart Permutt

Samuel French — London
www.samuelfrench-london.co.uk

ISBN 978-0-573-03024-6

www.samuelfrench.co.uk
www.samuelfrench.com

---

### FOR AMATEUR PRODUCTION ENQUIRIES

#### UNITED KINGDOM AND WORLD
#### EXCLUDING NORTH AMERICA

plays@samuelfrench.co.uk

020 7255 4302/01

Each title is subject to availability from Samuel French, depending upon country of performance.

---

## ONE LAST CARD TRICK

First performed at the Watford Palace Theatre on 2nd March 2006 with the following cast:

| | |
|---|---|
| **Magda** | Amanda Boxer |
| **Hetty** | Avril Elgar |
| **Sophie** | Gillian Hanna |
| **Loretta** | Debra Penny |

Directed by Lawrence Till and Stephan Escreet
Designed by Martin Johns
With special thanks to Paul Sirett

# CHARACTERS

**Magda**, early seventies
**Hetty**, late seventies
**Sophie**, late seventies
**Loretta**, forty-seven

The action of the play takes place in the kitchen and club room of a Friendship Club in the basement of a synagogue in London's West End

Time — Early July to late November 2000

## SYNOPSIS OF SCENES

# GLOSSARY

**bubba** (*booba*): grandmother
**Chanukah** (*Hanukah*): the Festival of Lights lasting for eight days and cleebrating the driving of the Syrians out of Israel and the reclaiming of the Temple of Jerusalem. It is traditional to give presents at this time and to light the candelabrum (see **menorah**)
**jahrzeit**: the anniversary of a death
**kam herein** (*kim herine*): come here
**kayn anahoreh** (*k-nay-n-horrer*): literally "It shouldn't be otherwise." It's a way of warding off evil spirits, so that everything is good.
**kugel** (*koogel*): a cake
**latkas**: potato cakes
**lockshen**: vermicelli
**le voyer**: a funeral
**maven**: an expert
**meshugas**: madness
**Oi Vey!**: Oh my God!
**Rosh Hashanah**: the Jewish New Year
**schickser**: a non-Jewish woman
**schmendrick**: an idiot
**schmutter**: a piece of old cloth or rag. Used sometime in the rag trade to describe a piece of material, i.e. "a nice piece of *schmutter*"
**Schwartzer**: a black person. Not derogatory
**shiva**: funeral prayers that take place in the mourner's house after the funeral
**shlepp**: to drag. A **shlepper** is someone who does a menial job for a living or someone who literally drags customers from the street into a shop
**shnorrer**: a beggar
**shul** (*shool*): a synagogue
**Torah**: the Five Books of Moses
**Was sagst du?**: What are you saying?

# KALUKI

The rules of the card game Kaluki are described in *Card Games Properly Explained* by Arnold Marks, published by Right Way; they can also be found on several websites including www.pagat.com

In memory of
Phil and Cissie Permutt

## COPYRIGHT MUSIC

# ACT I
## Scene 1

*The kitchen and club room of a Friendship Club of a synagogue in London's West End. Early July 2000. Mid-morning*

*On one side of the stage is the kitchen area and on the other, the club room which is the larger section, the main acting area. There is a window (currently open) with a broken catch in the wall of the club room and a door leads from this room to another unseen space. In the club room chairs and baize card tables are stacked against the walls and there are open cupboards full of games. There are paintings on the wall, perhaps a Chagall reproduction and a painting of the Sea of Galilee. There is also a wall clock. The kitchen has a large old-fashioned oven, a sink, a fridge, chairs and kitchen units*

*The Lights come up. The rooms are empty*

*Loretta enters through the door. She is forty-seven. She is slim with a mass of auburn hair and dark Semitic features. She is dressed rather carelessly in an old cardigan, dowdy blouse and plain skirt*

**Loretta** (*to someone off stage*) Mrs Isaacs, I'll be back in a minute. ... Bingo's next week. We can't have bingo without Hazel, Mrs Isaacs. ... There's no-one to call. ... Stanley can't call. ... Don't worry, Stanley will be here soon. ... He must have missed his transport. ... I'll find out ... (*She looks at the clock on the wall*) Oh my God, they'll be here any minute. (*She collects one of the tables from the corner, drags it across the room and sets it up during the following*)
**Sophie** (*off*) Lilly, we've got cream cheese sandwiches today. It's the cheddar that gives you heartburn.

*Sophie enters. She is a robust matron in her late seventies wearing a colourful summer two-piece and a pair of horn-rimmed spectacles. She is carrying a large bag or holdall*

Mrs Isaacs' looking very frail.
**Loretta** She insisted on coming.
**Sophie** Loretta you shouldn't be doing this. Where's Mr Katz?
**Loretta** He's got a double hernia. (*She closes the window*)

**Sophie** I must get him to mend that catch on the window.

*Loretta gets two packs of cards from a drawer and puts them on the table; she puts a cup there too*

**Hetty** (*off*) Lilly, I can't stop now, we've got a game on.

*Hetty enters. She is a vibrant slender woman in her late seventies, whose only concession to old age is that she walks with a stick. She is casually dressed in a cardigan and slacks and carries a handbag*

If I talk to Lilly longer than five minutes I feel like a wrung-out bit of *schmutter.*

*Loretta busies herself getting everything ready during the following*

**Sophie** She can't help it.
**Hetty** (*to Sophie*) I thought you'd deserted me.
**Sophie** I left you on the toilet, that's all.
**Hetty** Didn't you hear me scream?
**Sophie** Down here you couldn't hear a hyena scream.
**Hetty** The lock in the ladies upstairs has got caught again; I thought I was trapped. I was yelling the place down. No-one came.
**Sophie** Remind me to tell Mr Katz.
**Loretta** Hallo Hetty ... I must get that glass of milk for Mrs Isaacs. She's upset there's no bingo ... (*She rushes into the kitchen, mumbling to herself, finds a glass, pours out a glass of milk from a bottle in the fridge, then rushes back into the club room*) Back in a minute ...

*Loretta exits*

*Hetty and Sophie sit at the table*

**Hetty** Watching her is making me giddy.
**Sophie** She's been like this since Jean died.
**Hetty** She's always been like this. She can't sit still for two minutes. No wonder she's never picked up the game.
**Sophie** I'm still teaching her ...
**Hetty** She'll never get the hang of it ... I must have explained the rules to her at least a dozen times. A child of six could pick it up quicker. She's got the attention span of a gnat. She must be going through the change.
**Sophie** Hetty, she's not going through the change.
**Hetty** How can you be so sure?

**Sophie** She went through the change last August Bank Holiday ... Don't you remember? One minute she was hot, next minute she was cold and then it was all over.

**Hetty** That was quick.

**Sophie** Everyone's different.

**Hetty** Sophie, if I find out you know something I don't know I'll never tell you anything again.

**Sophie** I know nothing.

**Hetty** When it suits you ... Anyway, where's Magda?

**Sophie** She's got a tidy walk, she's got to go from Weymouth Street.

**Hetty** She doesn't walk, she takes a taxi.

**Sophie** If it's raining she takes a taxi, if it's fine she walks.

**Hetty** It can be pouring with rain or it can be a beautiful summer's day, she still takes a taxi. Am I right or am I right?

**Sophie** I know for a fact she only takes a taxi when it rains.

**Hetty** Then how do you account for the fact that a fortnight ago ——

**Sophie** When I couldn't get out because of my back ——

**Hetty** It was a boiling hot day ——

**Sophie** It wasn't that hot.

**Hetty** How do you know ? You were stuck indoors.

**Sophie** I can still feel the air ... Anyway, my neighbour downstairs went to the grounds that day in a short-sleeved blouse and a blazer and she was freezing cold.

**Hetty** If you're referring to Marie Eidelman, put her in the Sahara Desert and she'd still be cold ...

*Loretta enters in a rush, heading for the kitchen*

**Loretta** Stanley's feeling sick. I told him to put his head between his knees ... Lilly won't sit next to Mrs Isaacs.

**Sophie** Why?

**Loretta** She says she's got the evil eye.

**Sophie** They're worse than children.

**Hetty** Loretta, remember how hot it was a fortnight ago.

**Loretta** Yes, we had a heatwave. Must get Stanley a glass of water. (*She goes into the kitchen and fills a glass with water from the tap*)

**Hetty** What I'm trying to say is it was a boiling hot day and Magda took a taxi and she gave me a lift practically to my front door.

*Loretta rushes through the club room with the glass of water and exits*

**Sophie** I know Magda; she would never take a taxi on a day like that. She felt sorry for you and she wanted to give you a lift. So she took a taxi.

**Hetty** Why should she feel sorry for me? Nobody should feel sorry for me.

Do you think I'm such a *shnorrer* I have to have lifts in other people's taxis?
I can afford my own taxis, thank you very much.

**Sophie** Hetty, no-one's calling you a *shnorrer*.

**Hetty** You see how I spoil my grandchildren. They get presents on their
birthdays and Chanukah and Christmas. I never go empty-handed, so how
can you call me a *shnorrer*?

**Sophie** Hetty, you're getting hold of the wrong end of the stick.

**Hetty** Whenever I come to you I'm laden with stuff — cakes, biscuits — and
she's calling me a *shnorrer*.

**Sophie** All I asked you ever to bring is your appetite ...

**Hetty** If you're looking for *shnorrers*, go downstairs and see Marie
Eidelman. She sits in the library all day long in a thick jumper to save on
her fuel bills.

*Magda enters. She is a very elegant woman in her early seventies,
beautifully dressed in a well-cut suit and carrying a handbag. She speaks
with just the slightest trace of a German accent. She looks younger than her
years. She hangs her coat up and sits at the table*

**Magda** It was such a lovely day I thought I'd walk here.

**Sophie** Sure. (*She gives Hetty a triumphant look*)

**Hetty** Maybe now we can start.

**Magda** Where's Loretta?

**Hetty** Rushing in and out; she's making my head go round.

**Sophie** We should wait for her.

**Hetty** Why?

**Sophie** She likes to watch. I promised Jean I'd teach her the game.

**Hetty** She's been watching for years.

**Magda** She's such an intelligent girl.

**Sophie** She is an intelligent girl.

**Hetty** No, she's not, she's a dunce.

**Sophie** Hetty, they wouldn't have made her Assistant Cashier if she was a
dunce.

**Hetty** Yes, they would. It's her uncle's firm ... Assistant Cashier is another
word for a dogsbody ... She left school when she was fifteen with no
qualifications.

**Sophie** Jean took her out of school because the other girls were bullying her,
that much I do remember.

**Hetty** She couldn't get a job.

**Sophie** She had a bit of a breakdown.

**Hetty** Never heard of anyone having a breakdown for seventeen years.

**Sophie** They found the right pill for her complaint and now she's better.

**Hetty** She's not better.

**Magda** What exactly did the doctors say was wrong?

**Sophie** Jean was never very forthcoming about things like that, as you well know. What it all boiled down to is that Loretta had bad nerves.

**Hetty** She makes my nerves bad.

**Sophie** I thought when Jean died she'd have to go back into hospital. But she seems to be coping. That little job she's got is a godsend.

**Magda** Loretta is very good with figures.

**Sophie** She's been helping Mr Katz upstairs with the *shul*'s book-keeping while Barbara's been ill.

**Hetty** She's got no business being alone in that office with that man ...

**Sophie** Mr Katz is a very responsible man, he wouldn't be in that position otherwise.

**Hetty** I'm a very good judge of character; I always have been. When I was working for that firm of solicitors, Weinburg, Perlmutter and Smith, the minute a client walked into the room I knew right away whether he was guilty or not. They didn't want to let me go. And I'm telling you that Mr Katz is a wolf in sheep's clothing.

*Loretta enters*

**Loretta** Hallo, Magda, you look lovely. I really like that suit.

**Magda** Oh — it's so old.

**Loretta** Mrs Isaacs won't play Scrabble today but she was perfectly all right talking to Stanley until Lilly started crying.

**Hetty** Once she starts crying she never stops.

**Loretta** I left her in there. Thing is she's upsetting everyone, not only Mrs Isaacs.

**Sophie** You can't stop her coming.

**Loretta** If she starts screaming I'll have to go back in.

**Hetty** They should put her in a home.

**Sophie** Hetty, don't say things like that.

**Hetty** She's mad!

**Sophie** I remember Lilly when she and her husband had that butcher's in Charlotte Street ... Everybody went there, the Wolfsons, all the gown and coat people ...

**Magda** (*taking a package out of her bag and moving to Loretta*) Before I forget. I bought this for you, Loretta. (*She hands Loretta the package*)

**Loretta** Magda, you shouldn't.

**Magda** I couldn't resist it. I was in Fenwicks. It's just a scarf but it's your colouring.

**Loretta** Magda, you mustn't keep doing this.

**Hetty** (*aside, to Sophie*) She's easy to buy for, she's got nothing. (*To everyone*) Are we having a game or we just passing the time of day?

**Sophie** You'd better shuffle. I can't with my bad wrist.

*Magda sits at the table*

**Hetty** Give them to me. (*She takes the cards and shuffles them*) Shall I deal?
**Sophie** If Hazel's not here, you might as well.
**Magda** When's she coming back?
**Sophie** Originally she was only going for a long weekend for her grandson's wedding ——
**Hetty** — in Florida ——
**Sophie** — but you know Hazel, her idea of a long weekend can turn into weeks, months even … Meantime, she's left me in charge.
**Hetty** Since when?
**Sophie** Hetty, I've always been Hazel's second-in-command.
**Hetty** That's news to me … Shall I deal?
**Sophie** You just said you would. (*She gives Magda a worried look*)
**Hetty** No I didn't, I'm asking you now. Why would I ask you now if I'd asked you before?
**Sophie** Hetty, just deal.

*Hetty deals thirteen cards to each player during the following — cheat the number of cards if this takes too long. Magda gets a jack, queen and king in the same suit and three cards with the number four, each in a different suit*

**Hetty** I'm dealing. Do you want to hear a funny story?
**Sophie** Finish dealing, then we'll hear the story.
**Hetty** (*to herself*) She's trying to make out I don't know what I'm doing. That way I'll lose the game.

*The cards are now dealt. Hetty, Magda and Sophie get out their little purses and put some five p coins in the cup. Loretta gets out a pad and pen and paper from a cupboard to keep the score*

**Sophie** You've given me a lousy hand.
**Hetty** Every day's a fishing day but not every day's a catching day … I must tell you a funny story.
**Sophie** Not now, we're concentrating.
**Hetty** This fella, he wasn't a Yiddisher fella, goes to see his doctor and the doctor said: "I'm terribly sorry, you've only got six months to live …"
**Sophie** She's here again with her stories …
**Hetty** The doctor said: "Are you single?" The fella said: "Yes." The doctor said: "If I were you I'd get married straight away, only marry a Jewish girl." … "Why does it have to be a Jewish girl?" asks the man. The doctor says: "It'll seem longer."

*Nobody laughs; they've heard it before. Magda puts the six cards mentioned
above on the table*

**Sophie** I can't concentrate with Hetty telling stories all the time.

**Hetty** I was put on this earth to speak and when I can't speak I'll be dead.

**Sophie** Every time she throws down she leaves me with a load of cards I can't
get rid of. If I could see the cards properly I'd enjoy the game more.

**Hetty** For somebody who can't see, meantime last week — *kayn aynhoreh*,
she won every game.

**Magda** Are your eyes not getting any better, Sophie?

**Sophie** Every day it gets a bit darker. They think they can save my one good
eye, but I've got to wait.

**Hetty** You can be waiting forever these days.

*There is a scream, off*

**Loretta** That's Lilly. I'll have to go.

*Loretta rushes off*

**Magda** I went to see *Der Rosenkavalier* last night.

**Hetty** Any good?

**Magda** Kiri Te Kanawa was singing the Marschellin. She was simply
marvellous.

**Hetty** I'd go but all that singing gives me a headache.

**Sophie** (*to Hetty*) Her son gets her tickets, he did some surveying work for
them. Otherwise she couldn't go.

**Magda** I saw it in Berlin when I was only seven years old. My father took
me. Everybody wore gold and silver and the stage was draped in muslin;
the effect was stunning. Schwarzkopf sang like an angel. I wanted to rush
on to the stage and kiss her. It would have been better if I'd have spat in her
eye. (*She suddenly puts all her cards down on the table*)

*Loretta enters in a rush*

**Loretta** I managed to stop her screaming but now she feels faint. (*She looks
down at the card table*) You've won.

**Hetty** You know what they say, money goes to money.

*Hetty and Sophie hand Magda five pence each from their purses*

**Magda** If Lilly's feeling faint we'd better get her home. Is there anyone to
look after her?

**Loretta** A carer comes in twice a day. Her daughter doesn't live that far away.

**Hetty** She doesn't care.

**Magda** Loretta, let me talk to her.

*Loretta and Magda exit*

**Hetty** Look at her! Mother Teresa of Calcutta!

**Sophie** Those sandwiches won't get made on their own

*Hetty and Sophie move into the kitchen; they make sandwiches during the following*

**Hetty** What are you having tonight?

**Sophie** I got a quarter chicken in the fridge.

**Hetty** And?

**Sophie** Fresh fruit. And you?

**Hetty** Kippers.

**Sophie** And?

**Hetty** Dates.

**Sophie** Dates are good.

**Hetty** Dates are marvellous! ... Is Magda staying?

**Sophie** Your guess is as good as mine.

**Hetty** She won't stay. Our lunches aren't good enough for her. You've got to remember she's "one of those ladies who lunch".

**Sophie** Hetty, can you keep a secret?

**Hetty** You've known me all your life — of course I can keep a secret.

**Sophie** I'm going to tell you something that nobody else knows, and I don't want anyone else finding out.

**Hetty** If it's about Loretta having an affair with Mr Katz, I already know.

**Sophie** She's not having an affair with Mr Katz!

**Hetty** I've seen the look in his eye, double hernia or no double hernia ...

**Sophie** It's not about Loretta and Mr Katz, it's something much more serious.

**Hetty** What could be more serious than that. He's such a *schmendrick*. I don't want her throwing herself away on that man. She could be my daughter.

**Sophie** Hetty, this doesn't come easy.

**Hetty** So tell me.

**Sophie** I was in the corridor earlier. I overheard Mr Katz talking to Marcus Posner.

**Hetty** Who's Marcus Posner?

**Sophie** What do you mean, who's Marcus Posner? ... He's Chairman of the Board, that's all ...

**Hetty** What board?

**Sophie** The Board of Governors for the synagogue.

**Hetty** Oh, that board.

**Sophie** I don't know how to tell you.

**Hetty** You don't have to tell me. Streatham's chock-a-block. So all new burials are going to Cheshunt.

**Sophie** Since when?

**Hetty** It's common knowledge.

**Sophie** Not to me. Hetty, I'm not entering into a discussion about where we're getting buried; I've got something more urgent to tell you.

**Hetty** What's more urgent than that?

**Sophie** They're selling our *shul*.

**Hetty** You're making it up.

**Sophie** Would I make something like that up? I wish I was. Marcus Posner said he'd had an offer he can't refuse.

**Hetty** You weren't hearing right.

**Sophie** Hetty, it's my eyes that are bad, anyway I had my ear cupped right to the door. I didn't miss a word.

**Hetty** They won't sell.

**Sophie** You're not going to like this … They've had an offer from that fella who owns all the strip joints — what's his name? — Mike Stringer …

**Hetty** They'll never sell to him.

**Sophie** This is a prime site. Everyone's after it.

**Hetty** They won't sell to him. This is a holy place.

**Sophie** It's a millstone round their necks. There's hardly any members left. Everyone's moved away. People only keep it up for the burial.

**Hetty** They won't sell.

**Sophie** Anyway Marcus Posner was saying they can't afford the insurance any more. One way or another this building's costing them a fortune. Don't tell anyone. Not Loretta. Not Mrs Isaacs. Not Stanley. Not Lilly. Come Tuesdays they'll have nowhere to sit. If I can't play Kaluki my life wouldn't be worth living.

**Hetty** They won't sell.

**Sophie** Hetty you're sounding like a gramophone needle that's got stuck in the middle.

**Hetty** They wouldn't do it to us. Don't worry, Sophie, it won't happen. Rumours were flying around a few years ago. Remember when we had that spate of IRA bombings, and then it all went quiet? Not in our lifetime it won't happen.

**Sophie** Maybe I can have a word with that Marcus Posner.

**Hetty** What are you going to say?

**Sophie** He can't just pull down a synagogue.

**Hetty** I knew Marcus Posner when he was in short trousers. His mother was a buttonhole-maker.

**Sophie**  Her and Mrs Kowalski.

**Hetty**  She was also a buttonhole-maker.

**Sophie**  They used to sit in the window waving to us when we were coming home from school.

**Hetty**  And when our mothers died we kept in touch with them.

**Sophie**  We'll go and see this Marcus Posner and tell him we're not taking this lying down. It'll kill Mrs Isaacs, that's what it'll do. Her whole week is geared round coming here. This'll be the final straw with Lilly.

**Hetty**  That Mr Katz is behind all this. Before he came nobody thought of selling anything.

*Loretta and Magda enter*

*Sophie motions to Hetty not to say a word*

**Magda**  Lilly's fine now. I sat and held her hand and she was perfectly all right.

**Hetty**  I'll give you a medal.

**Magda**  She's looking forward to her lunch. Please don't make anything for me. I'm having lunch with an old friend. I haven't seen her for ages; we will have so much to catch up on

**Loretta**  I can't stay either. I promised I'd be at work this afternoon …

**Sophie**  They're keeping you busy.

**Loretta**  I've been promoted. I'm in charge of taking all the cheques to the bank every day. I couldn't do it when Mummy was alive. I had to be at home by three.

**Hetty**  You've got more time to yourself now.

**Sophie**  Hetty!

**Hetty**  It's not always a good thing for children to live at home with their parents. Mine fled the nest when they were still teenagers.

**Magda**  Before I knew where I was my son had left home and gone to university.

**Sophie**  If I had children I'd always want to live with them.

**Hetty**  Just as well you didn't.

**Sophie**  You'd better take these sandwiches through. Mrs Isaacs likes to be home before one.

*Hetty realizes she has gone too far and is about to apologize, but then just picks up a plate of sandwiches and exits*

She doesn't mean what she says. She thinks I don't know what's wrong. I've known her all my life and she thinks I don't know what's wrong. In three days time it'll be her daughter's *jahrzeit* … She died eight years ago and she thinks I don't know what's wrong ... A sailing accident — she was only thirty-eight.

**Magda** You don't get over a thing like that; that's why I make allowances.

**Loretta** I knew she had a daughter that died ... Mummy would never tell me.

**Sophie** She doesn't talk about it even to me but her neighbour hears her screaming every night ... Her son's in Canada. Loretta, can you take the rest of the sandwiches through for me?

*Black-out*

SCENE 2

*The same. A fortnight later; mid-July. Mid-morning*

*Hetty, Magda and Sophie are in the middle of a game. They each have their handbags with them. Loretta is keeping the score*

**Loretta** Hetty you can only hold fourteen points.

**Hetty** (*surveying her hand*) She's given me all pairs and no apples.

**Magda** I've got three cards left.

**Loretta** Lilly's very quiet today. She's just sitting there, I can't get a word out of her.

**Sophie** That's not like Lilly.

**Loretta** I'll just pop through. Magda, can you keep the score?

**Magda** Of course.

*Loretta exits*

**Hetty** Did you watch Channel Four last night?

**Sophie** I don't like Channel Four, it's too political.

**Hetty** They had a documentary on buggery.

**Sophie** Hetty!

**Hetty** I didn't know things like that went on. Did you, Magda?

**Magda** It doesn't interest me.

**Hetty** Funny, I thought you were a woman of the world.

**Magda** It's something I've never come across.

**Hetty** Didn't you and Max go to Tunisia one year? They do it in the streets there.

**Sophie** I've thrown down the wrong card again.

**Hetty** You should ask your son.

**Sophie** Hetty!

**Hetty** In some remote parts of Africa they do it as a means of contraception. I'm only quoting what they said in the documentary.

**Sophie**  I don't believe half of what they tell me in those documentaries. That's why I've stopped watching.

*Loretta enters and sits down*

**Loretta**  I can't get a word out of her. Stanley's sitting holding her hand.
**Sophie**  That's sweet.
**Hetty**  Loretta, I heard you talking to that Mr Katz as I was coming down the stairs this morning.
**Loretta**  I was helping him with the books.
**Hetty**  In the club room?
**Loretta**  He needed to ask me something.
**Magda**  Mr Katz is such a helpful man.
**Hetty**  He's a married man.
**Loretta**  He's not getting on with his wife.
**Hetty**  All this he told you?
**Loretta**  He wanted someone to talk to.
**Hetty**  I know the sort of man he is, one minute they want to talk next minute they want to do other things.
**Loretta**  Mr Katz is not like that.
**Hetty**  How do you know? ... I'm going to start arriving earlier in future so he won't be able to catch you on your own.
**Loretta**  He just wants to thank me for all my hard work — you know, while Barbara's been flat on her back.
**Sophie**  That's nice.
**Loretta**  He's asked me out.
**Hetty**  (*to Sophie*)  What did I tell you?
**Magda**  Where are you going?
**Loretta**  To a restaurant in St John's Wood.
**Hetty**  I was a virgin till I was twenty-seven.
**Sophie**  What's that got to do with anything?
**Hetty**  I was a good girl.
**Sophie**  We were all good girls.
**Hetty**  I waited till I got married.
**Sophie**  We all did in those days.
**Hetty**  Not like now.
**Magda**  What are you going to wear?
**Loretta**  I don't know.
**Magda**  I'll lend you something, we're practically the same size.
**Hetty**  Magda, I can't believe it, you're encouraging her to go out with a married man.                                                    .
**Loretta**  He and his wife aren't getting on.
**Hetty**  Does she know?

**Loretta** About what?

**Hetty** About you?

**Sophie** Hetty, he's asked the girl out, that's all.

**Magda** I have a beautiful silk jacket would look stunning on you. When are you meeting him?

**Loretta** Tomorrow night.

**Hetty** He didn't waste any time.

**Magda** Come round this evening and we'll choose the right outfit.

**Hetty** She's not a pauper, you know, she's got her own clothes.

**Loretta** Thank you, Magda, that's very kind of you.

**Magda** My pleasure.

**Hetty** Loretta, you're not going out with that man tomorrow and that's final.

**Sophie** Hetty, for God's sake she's not your daughter ... (*She realizes what she has said*) Hetty, I'm sorry ...

**Hetty** I know she's not my daughter.

**Sophie** Hetty, I opened my mouth without thinking.

**Hetty** Just because she's not my daughter doesn't mean I don't care.

**Magda** We all care.

**Loretta** I'm going out with Mr Katz.

**Hetty** So go, but don't come crying to me.

**Magda** Why should she come crying to you?

**Hetty** Sometimes I think that the lot of you were behind the door when common sense was given out. He's a married man, his marriage is over, he sees a young girl ...

**Loretta** Hetty, I'm forty-seven.

**Hetty** Biologically you may be, but in your head you're not ... It'll end in tears ...

**Sophie** You made me throw down when I should have picked up.

**Hetty** Don't blame me for everything that goes wrong in your life.

**Magda** I've just remembered my son is taking me out tonight. He wants me to meet his new friend.

**Hetty** Friend: what kind of friend?

**Magda** My son has lots of friends.

**Hetty** We know.

**Magda** He always likes me to meet them. This one's a lawyer. They're taking me to the opera. I shall have to wear something special. I can't let him down. Loretta, can you come round tomorrow instead?

**Loretta** I can come straight after work.

**Magda** That would be nice.

*They continue playing in silence*

**Hetty** Did you know Little Red Hiding Hood was a Yiddisher girl?

**Sophie** Hetty, we're having a game of Kaluki.

**Hetty** Sorry I thought we were playing tennis ... Anyway Little Red Riding Hood was going to see her grandmother — the *bubba* — in those warden-controlled flats on the other side of Hyde Park. She was beautifully dressed in a gingham frock with matching shoes and a red bonnet. She looked immaculate. Suddenly a big bad wolf came out from behind the bushes ——

**Magda** Do we have to listen to this ... ?

**Hetty** — and said to Red Riding Hood: "Where are you going, little girl?" "Actually I'm going to see my *bubba*. And in my basket I've got chicken soup, chopped liver and salt beef ..." "When I get hold of you I'm going to gobble! Gobble! Gobble! you up ..." And the big bad wolf chased her across the park. Finally she lost him and she's walking along and suddenly he comes from behind a tree and says: "Now I've got you, little girl, I'm going to gobble! Gobble! Gobble! you up!" ... "All this gobble! Gobble! Gobble! Doesn't anyone fuck around here?"

**Magda** (*aside; to Sophie*) She's getting so vulgar.

**Sophie** I'll have a word with her.

**Hetty** I heard that.

**Sophie** We didn't say anything.

**Hetty** I'm not the one who's vulgar. You should ask your son what he gets up to with that friend of his. Now that's vulgar.

**Magda** Hetty, that is none of your business.

**Hetty** You've no right calling me vulgar when I know what those boys get up to. It's not natural ...

**Sophie** Hetty, stop it ...

**Hetty** Her son's so marvellous ... Her son's done this — her son's taken her to this opera, that opera. Does she ever think about what they get up to when they're not at the opera?

**Loretta** (*looking at the score*) Hetty, you're out of the game.

**Sophie** Hetty, are you helping me with sandwiches or not?

**Magda** Don't make for me.

**Hetty** We know you're always too busy to eat with us.

**Magda** I'd love to, its just that I've got a million and one things to do.

**Hetty** Don't let us stop you.

**Sophie** Hetty, if they don't get their sandwiches on time, they'll start creating ... Magda, you have a nice day.

**Magda** Thank you, Sophie. Loretta, are you staying?

**Loretta** I'm not very hungry ...

*Magda and Loretta exit*

**Hetty** (*calling after Loretta*) You've got to eat!

*Hetty and Sophie move into the kitchen*

(*To Sophie*) She's got to eat!

*Sophie and Hetty prepare sandwiches during the following*

**Hetty** Jean wouldn't like Loretta going out with that Mr Katz.
**Sophie** Jean isn't here any more.
**Hetty** I promised Jean I'd look after Loretta.
**Sophie** We all promised Jean we'd look after her. Jean would be so pleased that she still comes here every Tuesday to lend a hand with the old people.
**Hetty** Jean would be calling a different tune if she knew she was going out with a married man. I don't know how his wife puts up with him. Every time I go into the office he's stuffing himself with food. He's got a drawer full of mouldy bagels.
**Sophie** Hetty, are you sitting down?
**Hetty** I am now. (*She sits*)
**Sophie** Do you want the bad news or the really bad news?
**Hetty** I've also got news.
**Sophie** Go on.
**Hetty** I wasn't going to tell anybody.
**Sophie** You can tell me, I'm your best friend.
**Hetty** You know that feller who owns all the strip joints?
**Sophie** Mike Stringer.
**Hetty** It was late last night, you know I have trouble sleeping. He'd parked his car right across the road from me. It was a cream and black Rolls Royce. I went straight downstairs in my nightdress.
**Sophie** Hetty, you didn't ——
**Hetty** I had my front door keys in my hand — there wasn't a soul about — and I gave that car a scratch right across the side.
**Sophie** Hetty, I don't know what's got into you lately; what if someone had seen you?
**Hetty** There was no-one about.
**Sophie** At your time of life you're turning into a criminal. I've got enough on my plate without having to visit you in prison.
**Hetty** They won't start putting me in prison. If anyone asks I'll say I had a mental block. At my age they're not going to argue with that. So what's the bad news?
**Sophie** I was in the office earlier. There was no-one there …
**Hetty** That Mr Katz must have gone off to the bagel shop …
**Sophie** I switched his computer on.
**Hetty** I wouldn't know where to begin.
**Sophie** My great-nephew taught me how to use one. A document came up on the screen ——

**Hetty**  Suddenly you're the MI5.

**Sophie**  — marked: "Synagogue Sale". Hetty, the deal with Mike Stringer's fallen through.

**Hetty**  I'm still glad I scratched his car.

**Sophie**  But there's been an offer from the Chinese Church.

**Hetty**  I've always got on very well with them.

**Sophie**  They're very nice people. I used to be friendly with a couple — they used to come into the shop — they were transvestites.

**Hetty**  I remember — you couldn't tell the difference.

**Sophie**  Prostitutes, but beautiful manners. Always said: "Mrs Green, how are you today?" First time they came in to try on dresses I said: "Go away and come again when there's a fella serving." But then we got pally and they ended up as my best customers. They asked me to go out with them to this pub in the East End.

**Hetty**  There's got to be somewhere for them to go, else they'd feel completely out of it.

**Sophie**  Phyllis Kershaw went out with them, I wouldn't …

**Hetty**  She'd go anywhere.

**Sophie**  They'd come into the shop full of customers and say: "Phyllis, what shall I wear tonight?" Her husband Ralph used to turn a blind eye.

**Hetty**  I couldn't bear him. I popped in one day, just to see you. He came right up and said: "Can I help you?" "I'm just looking." "If you want to look go to the fucking Tate Gallery."

**Sophie**  He was having an affair with the window-dresser, Norman.

**Hetty**  I never knew.

**Sophie**  We all kept quiet so as not to upset Phyllis.

**Hetty**  So what's the really bad news?

**Sophie**  We could all be out in the street in three months.

**Hetty**  Sophie, don't be daft.

**Sophie**  Hetty, I'm warning you. They'll the take the first offer that's on the table, their hands are tied behind their backs. I would have found out more but I heard footsteps on the passage.

**Hetty**  It's all rumours.

**Sophie**  Hetty, I saw the document.

**Hetty**  You misread it, you know how bad your eyes are.

**Sophie**  With my one good eye I can make out the letters well enough, thank you. But I've got news for them, we're not going without a fight.

**Hetty**  What are you going to do?

**Sophie**  We'll get a petition up. We'll write to our MP. Ring the local papers, the *Jewish Chronicle*.

**Hetty**  They won't let this place go. They won't be allowed. We've been coming here nearly forty years and before that we were in the old building in Manette Street. They can't take it away from us. I was so proud; my son had one of his paintings hung in the Ben Uri art gallery upstairs. I told everybody he was another Chagall ...

**Sophie** We'll make up banners and stand outside the town hall.

**Hetty** This place is important to a lot of people, not just us. I bumped into this actress while I was waiting for the lift — a yiddisher woman — she said she used to come here and do cookery classes ...

**Sophie** I don't remember no cookery classes.

**Hetty** Her name is Daphne Ringold and she's a famous cookery writer as well as an actress.

**Sophie** I don't remember no Daphne Ringold or no cookery classes. Unless she's related to the Ringolds who had that bakery in Dufors Place ...

**Hetty** Anyway she's rehearsing upstairs for this play for the Old Vic Theatre.

**Sophie** Very nice.

**Hetty** It's four hours long ...

**Sophie** *Oi vey!*

**Hetty** It's called *Crime and Punishment.* She said: "I'm the crime; I play an old woman who gets killed in the first twenty minutes. And the rest of the play's the punishment."

**Sophie** Talking of which you haven't paid me for the tickets.

**Hetty** What tickets?

**Sophie** We've booked the week after next to see "The Mazel Tovs" at the Brady Centre.

**Hetty** I've seen Danny Kaye at the Palladium. I've seen Anna Pavlova at the Golders Green Hippodrome.

**Sophie** I also saw that.

**Hetty** I've seen Mary Martin in *South Pacific.* So what do I want to see Moishe Chaim and Pipik in some lousy community centre.

**Sophie** Because the tickets are only five pounds. A coach is coming to pick us up and take us home. It includes a fish supper and a choice of desserts.

**Hetty** You've twisted my arm.

*Black-out*

SCENE 3

*The same. The following week; late July. Mid-morning*

*Magda, Sophie and Hetty are in the middle of a game. They have their handbags with them*

*Loretta enters through the door, in a rush. She is wearing a dress we haven't seen before with a cardigan over it and has books of raffle tickets with her*

**Magda**  I've got three cards.

**Loretta**  Will you buy some raffle tickets? They're only ten pence each or ten for a pound.

**Hetty**  That doesn't sound right.

**Magda**  Put me down for ten pounds' worth. (*She takes a ten pound note out of her purse*)

**Loretta**  That's very generous of you, Magda. That's ten for a pound so ten times ten is a hundred tickets … (*She tears off a huge wadge of tickets quite slowly*) Oh, thank you, Magda …

**Hetty**  I want to know what it's for before I start throwing my money around.

**Loretta**  A new bingo machine — the old one broke. It's the only thing that stops Lilly crying.

*Sophie gives Loretta two pounds*

**Sophie**  Give me twenty, darling … Ten for me and ten for Hetty.

**Hetty**  What are the prizes?

**Loretta**  Well there's a lovely Kenwood mixer donated by Mrs Isaacs — she's never taken it out of the box — a book by Clare Rayner ——

**Sophie**  I like her.

**Loretta** — "Everything Your GP Would Tell You If He Had The Time" — and a day-trip to Paris on Eurostar.

**Sophie**  Very nice.

**Loretta**  That was donated by Stanley's niece. She booked the ticket but then couldn't go because of her ——

**Sophie**  When is it?

**Loretta**  Sunday week … I must just nip out and get Mrs Isaacs a battery for her hearing aid.

*Loretta exits in a rush*

**Hetty**  I thought she was keeping the score.

**Sophie**  She's excited about the raffle.

**Hetty**  You mean she's excited about what's she's going to get up to with that Mr Katz. I feel quite ill at the thought of the two of them at it.

**Sophie**  She's very good with Lilly; she's got such patience.

**Hetty**  Lilly would try the patience of a saint.

**Magda**  Loretta's got a lot of patience; look how marvellous she was with her mother.

**Hetty**  She also had Alzheimer's.

**Sophie**  Jean did not have Alzheimer's.

**Hetty**  What do you mean she didn't have Alzheimer's!

**Sophie**  The doctor told me that if you can draw the face of a clock, then it isn't Alzheimer's. Jean had another type of dementia.

*Magda puts all her cards down on the table*

**Hetty** She's got Kaluki.

*Sophie and Hetty hand Magda the five p coins from the cup. Magda shuffles the cards*

**Magda** The secret is not to go down too soon.
**Hetty** (*to Magda*) Who's she trying to teach! You forget, it was me who taught you in the first place.
**Magda** No, I've been playing for years, Hetty. You never taught me ... I may have to stop coming soon altogether; my bridge club has moved to the morning.
**Sophie** We'll miss you.
**Hetty** No, we won't.
**Sophie** You can't play Kaluki with two.
**Magda** Hazel'll be back. Anyway Loretta's ready to play now.
**Magda** She looked so pretty when I dressed her up to go out last week. I brushed her hair, put it up. I dropped her off in the taxi outside the restaurant she was meeting him in St John's Wood, I was going that way. Mr Katz hardly recognized her.
**Hetty** And?
**Magda** And what?
**Hetty** Didn't you wait to see what happened?
**Magda** I wasn't going to spy on them, besides my son and his friend were taking me to a concert in Kenwood ...
**Hetty** If it was my daughter I wouldn't have let her out of my sight.
**Sophie** Hetty, she's forty-seven.
**Hetty** She doesn't act it.
**Sophie** She's not very worldly.
**Hetty** You can say that again.
**Magda** She looked radiant.
**Hetty** What she doing with a fat slob like that? He makes me sick.
**Sophie** Perhaps it's his mind.
**Hetty** What mind?
**Sophie** You get to a certain age you can't afford to be fussy.
**Hetty** I'd rather sit and watch paint dry than be seen out with that *schmendrick.*

*Loretta enters*

**Sophie** Did you get the batteries?
**Loretta** They didn't have the right size. So I got some tea bags.
**Hetty** What does she need a hearing aid for? She never listens.

**Magda** I was telling them how nice you looked when you went out last week.

**Loretta** Oh … Thank you. That silk jacket did it.

**Magda** You must keep it.

**Loretta** No …

**Hetty** Take it, she'll only give it to another pauper …

**Sophie** Did you have a nice meal?

**Loretta** We didn't have a meal.

**Hetty** What did I tell you? He's too mean to buy her a meal. I've met men like that before. Only I never gave in, did I, Sophie? We were good girls.

**Loretta** We just had a coffee. And a chat. He drove me home.

**Sophie** That's nice.

**Hetty** (*to Sophie*) She's not telling us everything. There was a documentary on last night about date rape.

**Sophie** Hetty, will you be quiet … ?

**Hetty** (*to Loretta*) Did he give you any drugs?

**Loretta** No, of course not.

**Hetty** If I find out he's done something he shouldn't have done, I'll make sure he's never capable of doing anything again.

**Sophie** What harm can he do her? He's got a double hernia.

**Hetty** Least if a fella asked me out we went to a Lyon's Corner House. We had egg mayonnaise and coffee — one and six …

**Sophie** That's a very pretty dress you're wearing today, Loretta.

**Loretta** Magda gave it to me when I came over last week.

**Magda** I bought in the sales last year, I'll never wear it.

**Sophie** Take the cardigan off, so we can see it properly.

*Loretta takes her cardigan off*

It's a lovely dress. Can you remember where you bought it, Magda?

**Magda** Some little shop off Bond Street.

**Sophie** Looks identical to one of the lines I used to sell at *Maison Netties*.

**Magda** I never shopped in Berwick Street.

**Sophie** Fichoux neckline with a pinched-in waist and a full skirt. I didn't know it had come back into fashion.

**Hetty** You'd have remembered if you'd shopped in Berwick Street; every time you walked past *Maison Nettie*, Sophie would be standing outside waiting to *shlepp* you in.

**Sophie** Hetty, I was never a *shlepper*! I was a saleslady — a *vendeuse*. Phyllis Kershaw was a *shlepper*.

**Hetty** She was the queen of *shleppers*.

**Sophie** Her husband Ralph was also a *shlepper*.

**Hetty** (*to Loretta*) I was standing there one day when two black women came in and he yelled out: "*Schwartzers*, get out the glitter!" … I didn't know where to look.

**Sophie** It was an unheard-of thing for a woman to leave Berwick Street with a full purse.

**Sophie** I was very good at sizing people up ...

**Hetty** You still are.

**Sophie** Customers would insist on trying on an outfit that was a size too small. They couldn't understand why it didn't fit. I never said a word.

**Hetty** She's making up for it now.

**Sophie** I used to say, "We've got one in your size, madam, put by for another customer; don't worry I can always get her another one." Then I'd quickly grab a bigger one from off the rail, take out the label and tell them it was their size. At the end of the day I could hardly speak, my mouth was full of labels.

**Hetty** Are we playing another game or not?

**Loretta** I must tell Mrs Isaacs about the batteries.

**Hetty** You're going nowhere.

**Magda** You'll have to count me out. I have to go home and pack.

**Hetty** Pack?

**Magda** My son is taking me to Cervia.

**Hetty** Cervia? Where's Cervia?

**Magda** On the Italian Adriatic, not far from Rimini, only much quieter. Max and I used to go there practically every year. We will be staying in the same hotel. A small family-run place but I know we will have five-star treatment. My son is going with his new friend Henry, such a charming young man. I said to them: "You don't want an old woman like me." But I'm going. They say the place hasn't changed at all. So I won't be here next week.

**Hetty** We'll survive.

**Magda** Or the week after. (*She gets up to go*)

*Loretta hands Magda her bag*

**Magda** Thank you, darling.

**Sophie** Have a safe trip.

**Magda** I must go. So much to do. You know how it is. I'll see you all when I get back.

**Sophie** Bye.

*Magda exits*

*The others look after her for a second before continuing their conversation*

**Sophie** What a son she's got. A chartered surveyor with his own offices in Mortimer Street. With children like that you don't have to worry about anything.

**Hetty** I knew her and Max when she was living in two rooms at the back of Marshall Street. Then he started earning and she moved over to the other side and now she thinks she's aristocracy.

**Loretta** I must go and see Lilly, then I said I'd go into work this afternoon — they're short-staffed. They know I don't usually work Tuesdays …

**Hetty** Not so fast. We want to know everything.

**Loretta** About what?

**Hetty** Last week.

**Loretta** You mean with Mr Katz? Nothing happened.

**Hetty** How could you go out with him?

**Loretta** Hetty, I like Michael, he's kind and considerate and he tells jokes …

**Hetty** As long as that's all he does.

**Loretta** He said how nice I looked. He held my hand under the table so nobody could see and he squeezed it a lot. Said he and his wife are getting a separation and then he'd start seeing me properly.

**Hetty** They all say that. Don't you believe it.

**Hetty** The Yanks used to promise us everything — stockings, chocolates — but we didn't give in. Marie Eidelman became a fallen woman for a couple of sirloin steaks …

**Sophie** Must you drag her into everything …

**Hetty** Now butter wouldn't melt in her mouth.

**Sophie** Did he tell you anything? Did you talk business?

**Loretta** We just talked.

**Hetty** We know you talked. We want to know about what.

**Loretta** Nothing much.

**Hetty** Did he mention the Chinese church?

**Sophie** Hetty, we were keeping that secret.

**Loretta** How did you know about that?

**Sophie** There's not much I don't know.

**Hetty** And what she doesn't know isn't worth knowing.

**Sophie** What else did he have to say?

**Loretta** Best coming from him.

**Sophie** You can't keep us in suspense, it's not fair.

**Loretta** He didn't say much at all, most of the time he was moaning about his wife.

**Hetty** We don't want to know about his wife.

**Sophie** If you don't tell us what is going on, I'm going to march right upstairs and ask him myself.

**Loretta** Well the board has agreed to the sale of the *shul*, they were about to exchange contracts, they must have done by now.

**Sophie** He's not said a word to us.

**Loretta** He doesn't want to upset you.

**Hetty** He's a horrible little man.

**Loretta** He tried to talk them out of it. He's going to be out of a job.

**Hetty** Who cares about him.

**Sophie** Have they definitely exchanged contracts?

**Loretta** I think so.

**Hetty** Something will go wrong at the last minute. Somebody will back down, they always do.

**Sophie** We'll make them back down.

**Loretta** Michael tried his best. Don't be angry with him.

**Sophie** So we're going to be sold off to the Chinese Church?

**Loretta** No, it's worse.

**Sophie** What do you mean worse?

**Loretta** Michael told me not to say anything.

**Sophie** Loretta it's us you're talking to.

**Loretta** I promised I wouldn't. The Chinese Church has fallen through. You're not going to like this..that Mike Stringer ...

**Sophie** Not the one with the strip joints.

**Loretta** He's come in with a better offer..we're talking over four million.

**Hetty** That'll fall through, four million or no four million ... Mind you most of them that come here wouldn't know whether they were praying to God or Phyllis Dixey!

**Sophie** Hetty!

**Loretta** I must go and see how Lilly is, she shouldn't be left.

*Loretta exits*

**Sophie** It'll kill Lilly if this places closes down.

**Hetty** She doesn't know where she is anyway. They should put her in a home. And Mrs Isaacs, the pair of them. They're over ninety — what do you expect? It's us I'm worried about. We've been members of this *shul* all our lives.

**Sophie** I know.

**Hetty** As kids we used to sit in the ladies' gallery and throw nuts and sweets after a *bar mitzvah*, and they want to turn it into a strip joint. If Rabbi Ferber was alive he'd drop dead ... He was a saint. And when I say a saint I mean a saint. When Rabbi Ferber walked down the street, everybody stopped and raised their hats to him. Jews, non-Jews, it didn't matter, even the tarts and the pimps ...

**Sophie** He had that air about him ...

**Hetty** I was never a religious woman, but he had that effect on me. He wouldn't let them close this place. If I didn't come here I'd be sitting at home staring at the four walls. Everyone's moving out of my block. Either that or they're dying. I don't know a soul. Lots of young families, but they don't talk to me. I didn't tell you I went into the wrong block the other day — the one across the road; it's identical — tried to turn the key in the lock when I realized ... A young Indian man with a turban answered the door. Very well-spoken. He took me right to my front door, because I didn't know where I was. He said I should have central heating put in. He told me I should get on to them to do it. He said my flat was like an ice rink and it's only September. They've been promising me central heating for years but I'm not going to let them in. My bills will go sky high. I couldn't even tell him my name. Isn't that how it all started with Jean?

**Sophie** It was a different thing altogether with Jean .You're just getting yourself into a state over the *shul*. Don't worry, darling, we won't let them pull it down.

*Black-out*

SCENE 4

*The same. One month later; late August. Mid-morning*

*There are several cardboard packing boxes in the club room. Magda, Sophie and Hetty are playing cards, their handbags at their sides. Loretta is busy putting everything from the room into the boxes*

**Magda** Cervia was simply marvellous. It hasn't changed since we were there last. Still just the same quiet elegant little resort for Italian families ...

**Hetty** You must have looked out of place then. A woman with two grown-up men ...

**Magda** Not at all, my boys were the talk of the hotel.

**Sophie** I've been trying to call you for days. Your phone was permanently engaged.

**Magda** You know how it is.

**Sophie** Anyway you're here at last. I've got bad news!

**Magda** It's not Lilly.

**Sophie** No, worse.

**Magda** Mrs. Isaacs!

**Loretta** Magda, you know you won first prize.

**Magda** What first prize?

**Loretta** In the raffle. The day-trip to Paris last Sunday.

**Sophie** On Eurostar.

**Hetty** Like she needs another holiday.

**Loretta** I didn't know what to do with it. You were in Italy ... They didn't want to go. I gave it to Lilly's granddaughter.

**Magda** How is Lilly?

**Loretta**  Didn't you hear? She had to go into a home. Only they wouldn't keep her. She's worse than Mummy was. They've put her in a mental ward.
**Sophie**  You're barking up the wrong tree. They've sold our *shul*.
**Magda**  Oh no!
**Hetty**  Mike Stringer wants to swap the Torah for a tart's tariff.
**Magda**  I've been a member of this *shul* since I came to England. I can't imagine not being here.
**Hetty**  Well, you'll have to start imagining.

*The three other women sigh. Loretta picks up a game of Scrabble and puts it in a large cardboard box*

**Hetty** (*to Loretta*) What are you doing with all those games?
**Loretta**  I'm just packing them away.
**Hetty**  What are you packing them away for?
**Loretta**  They said I could store them at work in the basement. Michael said we've got to be out of the building by Monday … Saturday will be the last Sabbos service.
**Hetty**  What are you talking about?
**Sophie** (*to Loretta*) Sssh … She hasn't taken it in. One minute she remembers, then she forgets.
**Magda**  In the meantime you can all come over to me on Tuesdays.
**Hetty**  I'm not *shlepping* to Weymouth Street. I'm staying here.
**Sophie**  I've tried to tell her. (*She puts her cards down on the table*)

*Magda hands over a coin to Sophie*

**Hetty**  Why is everybody whispering behind my back as if I'm some kind of idiot. What's going on?
**Sophie**  Nothing's going on … (*Aside to Magda*) She's taking it very badly. She relies on coming here.
**Hetty**  I can hear you, Sophie.
**Magda**  You're all coming to me next Tuesday … You too, Loretta.
**Loretta**  That'd be nice.
**Magda**  Just a moment … Next week isn't any good for me, because I'm making a little dinner party for my son and his friend Henry and his mother, then the following week they've asked me to keep the whole day free as the boys are planning a little surprise. I do hope I get on with Henry's mother. She has a horse and goes riding in jodhpurs every weekend in Suffolk. Henry says we're in-laws … Then the week after that is Rosh Hashanah …
**Hetty**  I'm not holding my breath.
**Loretta**  I can go back to working full time if I want to. I still want to keep Tuesdays free. That was my day for bringing Mummy here. I can visit Mrs Isaacs instead.

**Sophie** Mrs Isaacs is going to need a lot of support now. I mean she's virtually house-bound.

**Loretta** She wants to go and visit Lilly. Lilly's not allowed any visitors at the moment. They used to let me visit Mummy all the time.

**Hetty** How is your mother?

**Sophie** (*to Loretta*) She forgets ...

**Hetty** I saw her last week in the market ...

**Sophie** (*to Loretta*) Don't take any notice ... She'll realize in a minute.

**Hetty** First time I'd seen her in weeks, she'd lost weight but I didn't say anything. We went and had a cup of tea. I said: "Jean, don't be a stranger." She's very worried about you, Loretta.

**Magda** (*aside; to Loretta and Sophie*) She's delirious.

**Hetty** You go to work, you come home; you eat, you sit and then you go to bed. It's not natural.

**Loretta** We've been offered a room in Marble Arch.

**Hetty** Marble Arch!

**Loretta** It's not official, but Mr Katz told me.

**Hetty** She's here again with her Mr Katz.

**Loretta** He's going to come down later to discuss it with you.

**Hetty** Tell him not to waste his breath.

**Magda** Marble Arch is a very nice synagogue.

**Hetty** So you go there, I'm not stopping you.

**Loretta** They're giving us our own room for the *shul* which will seat up to a hundred and we can use their clubroom every Tuesday. They've got a lovely big kitchen; it'll be just the same.

**Hetty** No, it won't.

**Sophie** Marie Eidelman's a member of Marble Arch. I went to a wedding there once, it was all coral and pearl.

**Hetty** I'm not going to Marble Arch, I'm staying here.

**Sophie** I'm going to get a petition together. Everyone will sign. If I have to stand outside the town hall I will.

**Hetty** I'm not going nowhere.

**Sophie** I'll ring the *Chronicle*, we'll be on the front page.

**Magda** Don't get me involved.

**Hetty** I'm going nowhere. There's a memorial plaque to my Ruthie just as you come out of the lift.

**Magda** They can move it to Marble Arch.

**Hetty** My Ruthie's staying where she belongs, isn't she, Sophie?

**Sophie** Of course.

**Hetty** That Mr Katz is behind all this.

**Loretta** Mr Katz is a very kind man. He's doing all he can. At least it'll be somewhere for Mrs Isaacs to go on a Tuesday... and Stanley ...

**Hetty** He's getting a back-hander to shut this place. Well I'm telling you he won't get away with it.

**Loretta** Michael ... Mr Katz isn't like that.

**Hetty** And you've no right to be going out with him, a married man. I've a good mind to tell your mother!

*Loretta burts into tears and goes into the kitchen area*

**Sophie** (*coaxing Loretta back*) Loretta, come and keep the score.

*Hetty, Magda and Sophie put their cards down on the table. Loretta returns, sits down and counts the score*

**Loretta** (*counting Magda's cards*) Two ... four ... twelve ... (She counts Hetty's cards) Thirteen ... six ... twelve ... twenty-one ... twenty-six ... forty-one ... forty-seven. (*She continues counting under the following dialogue*)

**Magda** *Kayn anahorah*, you're playing well Sophie.

**Hetty** That's because you've been looking at my cards, so you knew what not to throw down.

**Magda** Hetty, Sophie would never cheat.

**Sophie** I can hardly see my own cards let alone yours. (*To Magda*) She's not herself. Whose turn is it to deal?

**Magda** Yours.

*Sophie deals during the following*

**Hetty** I'm watching you like a hawk.

**Magda** Take no notice.

**Hetty** My son was married here!

**Sophie** If all else fails I might have to resort to other tactics.

**Magda** What other tactics?

**Sophie** Don't worry, you'll be the first to know.

**Magda** Sophie, I don't know what you've got up your sleeve but don't expect me to join in.

**Loretta** (*reading the score*) Hetty, you've only got one life!

*The Lights fade to Black-out*

# ACT II
## Scene 1

*The same. About one month later. Evening*

*The work hasn't properly begun on the former club area yet. There are dust sheets everywhere. The pictures have been taken down. There may be evidence of workmen's tools etc.*

*When the Act begins, the stage is in total darkness. Then we hear the off-stage sound of two ferocious dogs barking*

**Sophie** (*off*)  Good boys, eat it up! You lovely boys!
**Magda** (*off*)  Sophie, be careful.
**Sophie**  (*off*)  They can't get out. Good boys, eat it all up for your Auntie Sophala.

*We hear the sound of slurping followed by mild yelpings of pleasure*

**Hetty**  (*off*) They've wolfed that down quick enough.
**Sophie**  (*off*) Thank you very much. Where would they have tasted chopped liver like that before?
**Hetty**  (*off*) Did you use garlic? I never did because Lou didn't like it.
**Magda**  (*off*) I use garlic in everything.
**Sophie**  (*off*) You don't want to make it too rich when you're feeding a dog.
**Magda**  (*off*) Did you put it in the blender?
**Sophie**  (*off*) This time I did, but I did crush in two weeks' supply of Soneral. Normally I just mash it with a fork — Alfred liked a coarse texture.
**Hetty**  (*off*) So did my Lou.
**Sophie**  (*off*) Pound of chicken liver to two hard-boiled eggs, one small onion — salt and pepper to taste. The secret ingredient is imitation chicken fat …
**Hetty**  (*off*) You mean *schmaltz* …
**Sophie**  (*off*) No, it's chicken fat without the fat. You buy it in jars.
**Hetty**  (*off*) I've never seen it.

*We hear the sound of snoring dogs*

**Sophie**  (*off*) What did I tell you? They're flat out. Magda … Come on …
**Magda**  (*off*) I'm not going near those dogs.

**Sophie** (*off*) They've got two weeks' supply of barbiturates in their stomachs, enough to knock out a single elephant. They won't be going anywhere.

**Hetty** (*off*) Sophie what if you've killed them?

**Sophie** (*off*) Don't worry I didn't give them that much ... Magda we're waiting. Hetty, take hold of my hand.

*We hear the sound of people moving downstairs*

*Sophie and Hetty enter through the window, Sophie supporting Hetty. Sophie is wearing protective gloves, has a miner's lamp strapped to her head, and carries a holdall, a carrier bag of food, a large box and two large portable lanterns. Hetty, warmly dressed, is carrying a holdall and a carrier bag*

**Hetty** I thought I wouldn't make it.

**Sophie** And God said "Let there be light." (*She switches on the lanterns*)

*Magda appears in the window; she is wearing a full-length mink coat. During the following, she drops a Fortnum and Mason hamper, a hair dryer, a large roll of toilet paper and her own personal valise through the window and then climbs in*

**Magda** We could all be arrested.

**Sophie** That window was already slightly ajar. The catch on it has been broken for ages. I told Mr Katz about it umpteen times. So we gained access to this building without force. Which means we're now legal occupants. I'm right, aren't I, Hetty?

**Hetty** She's right.

**Sophie** And she knows.

**Hetty** I didn't work for that firm of solicitors for nothing ... Anyway, why did we have to break in?

**Sophie** Because the place has been taken over

**Hetty** By who?

**Sophie** I've told you.

**Hetty** You didn't.

**Sophie** (*to Magda*) She'll remember in a minute.

**Hetty** There's nothing wrong with my hearing, you know.

**Sophie** I said we're going to be fine.

**Magda** We could have been savaged by those dogs.

**Sophie** They were like putty in my hands. (*Taking off the protective clothing, gloves and miner's lamp*) Remind me to return these to the barmaid at the *Flask*. The trick with dogs is to let them know who's boss.

**Hetty** (*to Sophie*) Since when are you a *maven* on dogs?

**Sophie** We always had a dog. Don't you remember? We kept it in the back
  yard.
**Hetty** You never had a dog. What sort of dog?
**Sophie** I don't know. A Heinz dog — fifty-seven varieties. Mummy used
  to talk to it in Yiddish; it understood every word. She'd say: "*Kam herein,
  Rex*" and he came …

*There is a noise at the window*

  Get on the floor.
**Loretta** (*off*) Hallo, it's only me. Are you there?
**Sophie** Loretta, you came.

*Loretta appears and climbs through the window carrying a large bag*

**Hetty** Left your Mr Katz then.
**Sophie** Hetty!
**Magda** (*to Loretta*) I'm so glad you're here, darling.
**Loretta** I wanted to come.
**Sophie** Loretta, darling, would you go and see if the stopcock is on. It's at
  the back of the Ladies'. Take a torch.
**Loretta** Of course.

*Loretta takes a torch from her bag and exits*

**Sophie** She wanted to come.
**Magda** More than I do.
**Hetty** So go … She's only frightened she's missing out on something.
**Sophie** It's the only answer. Hetty and I stood on the pavement with banners
  last week and we were told to move on. Maybe now they'll take notice.
**Magda** I promised the boys I'd go to the opera with them on Wednesday.
**Sophie** You're free to come and go as you please. Hetty and I are staying put.
**Magda** I haven't told Simon I'm here. He'd never allow it.
**Sophie** Magda, I didn't put a gun to your head and make you come. You said
  you wanted to be with us.
**Magda** I was worried about you. I couldn't let you do this on your own, such
  a hare-brained scheme. Besides I need to be here for Loretta.
**Hetty** Why?
**Magda** She needs me.
**Sophie** We can look after her.
**Magda** She relies on me.
**Hetty** Meantime whilst she's here we can keep an eye on her, make sure she's
  not gallivanting with that Mr Katz … She's still seeing him.

**Sophie**  Are you sure?

**Hetty**  I'm sure.

**Sophie**  Look, we're all here now and they can't get us out.

**Magda**  How long are you going to stay?

**Sophie**  For as long as it takes.

**Magda**  All I know is that it's freezing in here.

**Sophie**  By tomorrow they'll have to turn on the central heating and electricity.

**Hetty**  You've got a thick fur coat on. What are you worrying about? (*She goes over and feels the coat*) That's not a good quality mink. It's too heavy. I know what I'm talking about. A good mink coat should be light.

**Magda**  I'm not wearing my best clothes for sitting in some damp basement.

**Hetty**  This isn't a damp basement; it's our home.

**Magda**  Home! This isn't my home, Hetty. I have a beautiful warm home with a power shower.

**Hetty**  Go home then; we don't need you.

**Magda**  This charade is quite foolish; it will get you nowhere. It's best I go.

**Sophie**  Magda, don't go. Not yet. Stay for at least one night. We've got to show them we mean business. I've been planning this for weeks, you can't walk out on me now.

**Hetty**  Let her go.

**Magda**  Where will we sleep?

**Sophie**  Down here of course.

*Loretta enters*

**Loretta**  The toilet's working; I just used it.

**Sophie**  Good girl. Now, we don't want any intruders. (*She bolts the door at the back*)

**Hetty**  I should have brought my little portable TV; they've got a documentary on tonight about socially transmitted what's-its.

**Sophie**  We can get it tomorrow.

*Loretta busies herself unpacking the box, producing a kettle and two flasks*

**Sophie**  First things first; we can have a nice cup of tea.

**Hetty**  Thank God, I'm spitting flies here.

**Loretta**  I'll make it.

**Sophie**  (*handing Loretta a lantern*) Take it in the kitchen.

*Loretta takes some tea bags, powdered milk, sugar etc. from the box. Magda takes a cake out of the hamper*

**Magda**  I've got a walnut cake to go with our tea.

**Hetty**  Home-made?

**Magda**  No. I didn't have time.

**Hetty**  (*getting a cake out of her holdall*) Home-made honey cake.

**Sophie** (*getting a cake out of her holdall*) Home-made cheesecake with fresh cream cheese.

**Loretta**  I didn't bring a cake.

**Hetty**  So make the tea.

*Sophie, Hetty and Magda put their cakes on one of the dust-covers*

*Loretta goes into the kitchen area with the lantern and flask etc. She opens a cupboard where she finds some cups. She makes four cups of tea during the following*

**Loretta**  Everything's still here but it's all dirty.

**Hetty**  British workmen!

**Sophie**  Scald everything with hot water. If not, I've got paper cups.

**Hetty**  I made egg and onions, two cholas and I brought a jar of rollmops.

**Sophie**  I've got two whole chickens and a rice salad.

**Magda**  In my Glyndebourne hamper, I've brought latkas, borscht, kugel, gefillte fish in little jars, bagels with cream cheese and smoked salmon, quince marmalade, three dozen bridge rolls, two plavas from Grodzinskis, Piccadilly Piccalilli, a flask of Bloom's lockshen soup — and the leftover vol-au-vents from Melanie Karlofsky's *le voyer*.

**Hetty**  That's a peculiar mixture.

*Loretta returns with the four cups of tea on a tray and hands them round*

**Sophie**  Thank you, darling.

**Loretta**  The fridge isn't working.

**Sophie**  Well, it won't until they turn the electricity on.

**Loretta**  I don't have to make the tea at work any more. We've got a new office junior, Alan. Tomorrow I must pop back and see Mrs Isaacs, she won't touch the Meals On Wheels. I told her they were kosher.

**Sophie** (*looking at all three cakes*) You know, those cakes look so delicious I'm going to have to leave them all. You can wrap one of them up and take it round to Mrs Isaacs.

**Loretta**  Stanley's not been well.

**Sophie**  Stanley's got a sweet tooth. (*She wraps up her cake*)

**Loretta**  Lilly's still screaming on that ward.

*Magda wraps up her cake*

*We hear the sound of footsteps on the stairs. Sophie turns the lanterns off*

Ssssh … It's the security man, he doesn't normally come round for another half an hour.
**Hetty** How do you know?
**Sophie** Hetty, I planned this operation down to the last detail.

*There is a banging on the door. A beam of torchlight flashes under the door*

**Loretta** What are we going to do?
**Sophie** We're going to finish our tea and then we're going to have a game of cards.
**Loretta** He's going to break the door down.
**Sophie** I told you there's nothing he can do. We have our rights.
**Hetty** Suddenly she's sounding like a union official. All those years I was selling the *Daily Worker* at the corner of Tottenham Court Road and now she's talking about rights.

*We hear footsteps as the security guard moves away*

**Loretta** What if he tells Mr Katz?
**Sophie** So let him.
**Hetty** Loretta, you've been seeing him.
**Loretta** No … Only once.
**Hetty** I wouldn't let him near me, with that big fat stomach and that dirty greasy beard.

*Sophie produces two packs of cards which she places on the card table*

**Sophie** Hetty, do you want to deal?
**Hetty** Sure.

*They gather round the table for a game*

(*Shuffling and dealing the cards*) Do you want to hear a funny story?
**Sophie** She's here again with her stories.
**Hetty** This one's true. A Yiddisher couple got into a taxi outside Manchester airport.
**Sophie** She's never been to Manchester …
**Hetty** The wife can't speak any English, only Yiddish. And the taxi driver said: "Had nice holiday?" And the wife's going: "*Was sagst du? Was sagst du?*" "He asked us, Dolly, if we had a nice holiday?" Then the taxi driver said: "Where are you from?" "*Was sagst du?*" she's saying. "He wants to

know where we're from, Dolly." "Actually, we come from Wythenshawe
… I told him we come from Wythenshawe …" "Oh, Wythenshawe," said
the taxi driver, "I know it well; I had the worst fuck in my life in
Wythenshawe." *"Was sagst du?"* "He says he knows you!"

*Black-out*

SCENE 2

*The same. About ten days later; early October. Late afternoon*

*In the club room are: a large hamper with a big note on it saying: "With love
and support from the Oxford and Cambridge Club"; a flower arrangement
with a note which says "All the best from the Stanmore and District Ladies
Guild" and a large basket. There are a radio cassette player and some tapes
in the club room and cosy touches such as a tablecloth have been added. A
menorah stands on a table with one Chanukah candle burning in it. Each of
the women has some personal belongings in evidence*

*The electricity and lights are now working in both areas. The radio cassette
is playing Latin American samba music. Magda is trying to teach Loretta the
samba. Sophie and Hetty are preparing a meal. Hetty is reading a copy of the*
Jewish Chronicle

**Magda** It's easy … It's just hop together and back … Step … Hop
together …

*Loretta takes a few tentative steps*

*The Lights fade on the club room*

**Hetty** Front page of the *J.C.*
**Sophie** Didn't I say we'd make the front page of the *Chronicle*? If it had been
left to you and Magda we'd have still been sitting at home …
**Hetty** (*reading*) "The ladies of a Soho synagogue defy property developers"
… Front page …
**Sophie** The *Sunday Express* said we touched the heart of the nation. I've
had so many calls my mobile's been doing the quickstep.
**Hetty** Has that Mike Stringer called you?
**Sophie** Hetty, he hasn't stopped calling me. You heard his last message.
**Hetty** What does he want?
**Sophie** You know what he wants. He wants to offer us money to get out.
**Hetty** Let him stew.

**Sophie** He could offer us the crown jewels; we're not budging. And we're not being fobbed off by a room at Marble Arch either; this is our synagogue and we're staying here.

**Hetty** Anyway, we're enjoying ourselves. It's like being on holiday. Like when we all went to Goring-by-Sea ...

**Sophie** Lady Lilly Montague organized that ...

**Hetty** We had a lovely week's holiday ...

**Sophie** We did.

*They both burst into a tune from "Iolanthe"*

**Sophie** | (*singing*) | Happy are we in Goring-by-Sea
**Hetty**  |            | All in the big marquee to sleep in
                           Beds on the floor, washing out of doors ...

**Hetty** (*speaking*) Marvellous woman, that Lady Montague ...

**Sophie** She was a marvellous woman.

**Hetty** All those evening classes she had going ... I was the clever one so I studied foreign languages, public affairs, but you were a dunce ...

**Sophie** I wasn't a dunce. I won a scholarship to The Burlington School for Middle-Class Girls ——

**Hetty** You'd have been out of place there.

**Sophie** — but my mother couldn't afford the uniform. It was a blazer with a straw hat and gloves ...

**Hetty** You never won no scholarship, you were a dunce ...

**Sophie** Mr Moses Montefiore presented me with a Bible when I was twelve.

**Hetty** He knew you didn't have one ...

**Sophie** Lady Montague told my mother that I should have been on the stage. It wasn't a thing she said to everybody. I was in all her productions. You weren't.

**Hetty** I was busy studying, making something of myself.

**Sophie** I played Buttons in *Cinderella*. I carried Lavinia's train in *Titus Andronicus*. I was nine years old and one of the fathers came round and presented me with a pound box of chocolates which was quite something to give to a child.

**Hetty** Miss Lilly would have been very proud to know you ended up working in a dress shop.

**Sophie** What do you want, boiled or fried gefillte? I'm doing both ... On second thoughts I'm only doing boiled.

*The Lights cross-fade to the club room. The music stops*

**Magda** Shall I put another tape on?

**Hetty** (*from the kitchen area*) I love that Edmundo Ross.

*Magda puts on another tape; a Cha-cha-cha plays*

**Magda** It's a Cha-cha-cha. Come on, Loretta.
**Loretta** The girls at work go to salsa classes.
**Magda** You'll be ahead of them. I'll give you a quick lesson. My son loves dancing. So does his friend Henry. They're threatening to take me to one of their nightclubs. Now it's just one, two, cha-cha-cha, three, four, cha-cha-cha …

*The Lights cross-fade to the kitchen area*

**Hetty** She'll never get the hang of it, she's got no rhythm.
**Sophie** I went out with a boy with two left feet, he took me to the Astoria Dance Hall …
**Hetty** I never went to the Astoria.
**Sophie** You went with me.
**Hetty** I went to the tea dances at the Paramount. My mother didn't like me going to the Astoria because all the tarts used to hang outside.
**Sophie** We didn't bother them, they didn't bother us.
**Hetty** I stopped going to dances with you for one good reason, and for one good reason only — the minute my back was turned you used to steal my partners.
**Sophie** Do you want a green salad or shall I make some coleslaw?

*The Lights cross-fade to the club room. Loretta and Magda dance during the following, Loretta becoming increasingly confident*

**Magda** (*to Loretta*) Next time you go out with your friends they will be so impressed.
**Loretta** I saw Mr Katz last night.
**Magda** I know.
**Loretta** You know.
**Magda** You were so secretive about where you where going … I guessed.
**Loretta** I didn't want Hetty to know.
**Magda** Hetty is an interfering old bat. And getting more senile by the day. Anyway, tell me about last night.
**Loretta** He took me to a really nice Italian restaurant. I had tiramisu and then we went back to his place.
**Magda** What about his wife?
**Loretta** She's left him.
**Magda** Are you sure?
**Loretta** Oh, yes. He showed me her wardrobe, all her clothes are gone. I saw her photograph on the sideboard, a real hard-faced cow. Don't know how he could have lived with her.

**Magda**  He's no prize catch.
**Loretta**  He wants me to move in.
**Magda**  So soon.
**Loretta**  It's been four months. He's never done anything. Even when I was in his flat last night, he didn't try anything on.
**Magda**  Are you sure he's normal?
**Loretta**  He's a gentleman ... Only he doesn't want me to stay here any more. Said it's an embarrassment for the board. Three old women playing Kaluki. He said we'll never win.
**Magda**  He's probably right.
**Loretta**  He's lost weight. It's all the worry. He's still fat but not as fat. I like cuddly men.
**Magda**  Do you really like him?
**Loretta**  Of course I like him. I know he's a slob and untidy ...
**Magda**  He's much older than you.
**Loretta**  He's not. He just looks it.
**Magda**  Has he got a job?
**Loretta**  He's gone back to mini-cabbing ... Wants me to move in straight away.
**Magda**  What would your mother say?
**Loretta**  Mummy was always going on at me to find somebody ...
**Magda**  But Mr Katz!
**Loretta**  You don't know him. We sat on the couch, kissing and cuddling. I felt really happy. He said I needed lots of love and affection and he could give it to me. He's on the waiting list for his operation and then he'll be able to really make me happy.

*The music ends; Loretta finishes the dance with a big flourish*

**Magda**  You have friends at work ...
**Loretta**  They're nice, but they only talk to me when they have to ask me something — you know, about work — and I often see them huddled in corners and I know they're not talking about me. I mean I used to think everybody was — talking about me — but the doctor said it was my imagination and Mummy said people have got better things to do than talk about you. Then they go out, you know, after work, to a wine bar, and they don't ask me. They're all a lot younger ... But I can't say they're not nice. You see, Michael's the first man to take an interest in me in that way ... But that doesn't matter to me. You see, since Mummy and Daddy have gone ...
**Magda**  I know.
**Loretta**  It's been lonely in that flat with just me. That big long corridor and nobody there when I get in at night.
**Magda**  There must have been others.

**Loretta** Not really. There was one boy — Harold. We went out. I brought him home and Mummy and Daddy really liked him. But then he got engaged to someone else. I think they went to live in Gateshead. Her family is very religious apparently.

**Magda** You mustn't throw yourself at Mr Katz just because he happens to be there. You've got plenty of time.

**Loretta** But that's the trouble Magda, I haven't.

*The Lights cross-fade to the kitchen area*

**Hetty** Sophie ...

**Sophie** What is it, darling... ?

**Hetty** I think I've wet myself.

**Sophie** Come on, I'll take you to the toilet.

**Hetty** Last night I made the blankets all damp. I didn't want to tell anybody.

**Sophie** You'll have nice clean blankets tonight, don't you worry.

**Hetty** Suppose I make them wet again.

**Sophie** We'll cross that bridge later.

**Hetty** Sophie, I can't control myself no longer.

*During the following, Sophie helps Hetty to the door*

**Sophie** Now just hold on to me and you'll be fine.

**Hetty** Something's happened to my Ruthie.

**Sophie** Your Ruthie's fine ...

**Hetty** How would you know. You've never had children so you don't know what it's like.

*They unbolt the door and exit*

**Magda** Loretta, come back to my flat; we can't stay here any longer.

**Loretta** We can't leave Hetty and Sophie on their own. They're old.

**Magda** If they won't see sense ...

**Loretta** We're doing really well.

**Magda** We're a laughing stock. My son is furious with me.

**Loretta** But you come and go as you please ... I popped in to see Mrs Isaacs. She's not eating. She can't hear a thing. She wants to come here.

*A mobile phone rings. Magda searches in her handbag. Loretta searches in her large bag and eventually fishes out her mobile*

**Loretta** It's mine.

**Magda** I was expecting a call from my son.

**Loretta** (*on the phone*) Hallo. ... Yes. ... Where are you? ... Sorry, I can't hear you. ... I'll have to take it outside ... (*Putting her hand over the phone*) It's Michael ...
**Magda** I know.
**Loretta** I won't be a minute.

*Loretta exits out of the window*

*Magda looks through the pile of cassettes and tidies up a bit*

*Sophie and Hetty enter*

**Hetty** False alarm. I thought I wanted to go and when I got there I didn't.
**Sophie** The window's open ...
**Magda** Loretta just popped out for a minute. ... Someone rung on her mobile.
**Sophie** I hope no-one's ill.
**Hetty** Bad news travels fast.
**Sophie** I know.
**Hetty** Marie Eidelman bought a mobile and the first call she got was to say her sister had passed away. They hadn't spoken in over forty years.
**Magda** How ridiculous
**Hetty** I heard the story from both sides. Marie's sister had been frying fish all day. Marie came round and her sister gave her a lovely piece of plaice. And she said: "I don't fancy fish tonight." Her sister got annoyed.
**Sophie** So would I.
**Hetty** And says "If you don't eat it, I'm going to give it to the cat.". ..."Are you telling me you give me the same food as you give your cat?" With that Marie stormed out and they never spoke again.
**Sophie** That's Marie Eidelman for you.

*Loretta creeps back in through the window*

**Magda** So?
**Loretta** I've got to go.
**Sophie** Go where?
**Loretta** Michael — Mr Katz — he's not well.
**Hetty** Let him rot.
**Magda** What's the matter with him?
**Loretta** He's very upset.
**Hetty** So he should be.
**Loretta** He's waiting for me outside, he's just dropped someone off in Seymour Place.
**Magda** Do you want to go?

**Loretta** I've never known him so upset. He was crying on the phone.
**Hetty** My Lou never cried.
**Loretta** He said he might do something to himself.
**Hetty** That's the oldest trick in the book, isn't it Sophie?
**Sophie** It is.
**Loretta** He doesn't like me being here, he says it's not safe.
**Sophie** We're safer here than in our own homes
**Loretta** He needs me. He says if I don't come now then it's all over. (*She starts rummaging around for her few belongings*)
**Hetty** All right, then, go, but don't come back.
**Sophie** Hetty, she can come back whenever she wants.
**Loretta** (*gathering the last of her belongings*) Thank you.
**Magda** Ring me, darling, whenever you want. I don't care if it's three o'clock in the morning.

*Magda and Loretta hug. Loretta turns round to Hetty and Sophie*

**Hetty** You've made your choice, now get out!
**Sophie** Hetty!

*Sophie gives Loretta a hug*

*Loretta leaves through the window, closing it behind her*

**Hetty** She's a wicked girl, leaving us like that.
**Magda** She's in love, or she thinks she's in love.
**Hetty** So you're an expert on love then, are you?
**Magda** I was very happy.
**Hetty** Are you so sure?
**Magda** Hetty, what are you trying to say?
**Sophie** Nothing. She's saying nothing. Why don't we have a game?
**Hetty** There's no-one to keep the score.
**Sophie** We can keep the score. It'll take our mind off things. (*She gets the cards out*) Hetty, do you want to deal?
**Hetty** I'm not in the mood.
**Magda** Let me deal (*She shuffles the cards through the following dialogue*)
**Sophie** I had them on the phone this morning ...
**Hetty** Had who on the phone?
**Sophie** Channel 4.
**Hetty** What do they want?
**Sophie** They only want to make a documentary about us, that's all.
**Magda** My son would never allow me to be filmed.

**Sophie** Hold your horses, I said I'd get back to them.

**Hetty** Marie Eidelman had one of those film crews in once, when her nephew was had up for smuggling. She said they were everywhere; it was like the invasion of the body snatchers.

**Sophie** One way or another we've caused quite a sensation. Sooner or later they're going to have to give in. Everyone's on our side. Did you see that hamper of fruit from the Oxford and Cambridge Club? And that beautiful tropical arrangement from the Stanmore and District Ladies' Guild?

**Hetty** That basket from the pub can go right back.

**Sophie** Hetty, you can't do that.

**Hetty** Where's their sense sending a group of Yiddisher women two crates of beer and a box of pork scratchings?

**Sophie** They probably weren't thinking; they were in a rush to get it over. They don't know how long we're going to be here. (*She picks up a card from the table*)

**Hetty** (*to Sophie*) If your eyes are so bad how come you can see which card to pick up?

**Sophie** I can only just make out the cards. Soon it'll be total darkness.

**Magda** When are you having the operation?

**Sophie** I should be going in next week, but I can't leave you.

**Hetty** You could be waiting ages for another operation.

**Magda** It's not like it's an emergency.

**Hetty** What do you mean it's not an emergency? If you couldn't see it would be an emergency.

**Sophie** Hetty, please ...

**Magda** All I meant was ——

**Hetty** I know what you meant. It's all right for you, you can have an operation anytime you like.

**Magda** Hetty, all I meant was it's not a matter of life and death.

**Hetty** When you're losing your sight, let me tell you, it is a matter of life and death. Isn't it, Sophie?

**Sophie** Hetty, that's enough.

**Magda** (*putting her cards down*) I can't play in this atmosphere.

**Hetty** Atmosphere! You're the one creating an atmosphere. You think you're doing us a favour just by being here. You may be queen of the bridge club but here you're nothing ...

**Magda** It's all right, Hetty, you won't have to see me again ...

**Hetty** In fact you're less than nothing ...

**Magda** It has become quite claustrophobic us all living here.

**Sophie** You come and go as you please.

**Hetty** Sophie and I haven't budged.

**Magda** My son is very unhappy about me being here. His friend said he would never allow his mother to get mixed up with something like that.

(*She collects up her things during the following*) Anyway, we have tickets for the opera tonight. *The Italian Girl in Algiers*. It's the story of an emancipated European woman living amongst savages.

**Hetty** Boys that age should be going to football matches, not schmoozing at the opera.

**Magda** Cecilia Bartoli is singing Isabella for the first time. Henry — you know, Simon's friend — said she was born to sing Rossini. He knows so much about opera; he says she is a true coloratura mezzo. He saw Marilyn Horne's farewell performance in the same role.

**Sophie** You'll be coming back.

**Hetty** Let her go, she's wicked, that's what she is.

**Sophie** (*to Magda*) Don't take any notice, she's not herself.

**Hetty** She's an evil woman, that's what she is.

**Sophie** She's not herself.

**Magda** Hetty, I've always been a good friend to you. When you came crying to me saying you didn't have any vests for the children, I willingly gave you what I had. Then I saw you walking up and down the street in a new coat.

**Hetty** My husband made it for me.

**Magda** With a fur-lined collar.

**Hetty** It was the fashion. I never went to you for money. She's telling lies.

**Sophie** Don't listen to her, she'll have forgotten about it later ...

**Magda** Max always found Lou work.

**Hetty** My Lou was a marvellous tailor, wasn't he, Sophie?

**Sophie** Of course.

**Hetty** He could find work anywhere.

**Magda** Sometimes the work was late — not finished properly, the lapels not properly stitched.

**Hetty** Lou never sent in unfinished work. Max always employed lousy cutters.

**Magda** He was in Savile Row.

**Hetty** I don't care where he was. Lou would be up all night re-cutting the cloth. He never got extra.

**Magda** Max was a very generous man.

**Hetty** And we know where most of his money went.

**Sophie** Hetty, enough already.

**Hetty** She should know. Your husband was carrying on with that *schickser* from the *Blue Post*. It was common knowledge. She got pregnant but she got rid of it. Max saw to that. I thought: "Shall I tell her or shan't I tell her?" So now I'm telling you.

**Magda** I don't believe you.

**Hetty** Whenever anybody asked where Max was, he was always away on a long week-end. It became a standing joke.

**Magda** He went abroad buying.

**Hetty**  He never set foot outside Soho. He took a room above the pub and they'd carry on there.

**Hetty**  You want proof, I'll give you proof.

**Magda**  What proof? Why are you making all this up?

**Hetty**  If you don't believe me, ask Cyril Greenspan.

**Sophie**  What's Cyril Greenspan got to do with it?

**Hetty**  Weekends he worked behind the bar at the *Blue Post*. Cyril always carried a torch for me. He told me everything that went on. He remembers giving them the keys for the room upstairs on more than one occasion. Don't worry, they weren't the only ones that used to carry on up there.

**Sophie**  Who else?

**Hetty**  Nobody you know. I kept schtum at the time because I felt sorry for you, Magda, but now I don't.

**Magda**  She's talking utter rubbish.

**Hetty**  I'll give you Cyril Greenspan's number if you like. He's moved to Dollis Hill but he'll be only too pleased to tell you everything.

**Magda**  You've always been jealous of me.

**Hetty**  Why should I be jealous of you?

**Magda**  Because my husband had a successful business.

**Hetty**  Before he gambled it all away.

**Magda**  Because I live in a beautiful flat.

**Hetty**  You started off in two rooms like the rest of us.

**Magda**  Because my son is always taking me out. Tonight after the opera the boys are taking me to my favourite restaurant, *L'Escargot*. Max and I used to go there all the time when Elena was there. And next year the boys are taking me skiing.

**Hetty**  I hope you break your neck ...

**Sophie**  Hetty!

**Magda**  I should be angry, but I'm not. All this has proved too much for you. It was inevitable. I feel sorry for you.

**Hetty**  Sorry for me — why should you feel sorry for me? I had a husband that loved me, didn't I, Sophie?

**Sophie**  Of course.

**Magda**  That was the one thing about being married to Lou — he couldn't be unfaithful even if he wanted to.

**Hetty**  What exactly are you saying?

**Magda**  Hetty, he was hardly Engelbert Humperdinck.

**Hetty**  Lou was a marvellous man wasn't he Sophie?

**Sophie**  Sure.

**Hetty**  He gave me everything I wanted. We had two beautiful children. You idolized my children, didn't you, Sophie?

**Sophie**  I did.

**Hetty**  You couldn't have children so you idolized mine.

**Sophie** I did. They were like my children.

**Hetty** I cry in bed every night when I think about my daughter. That's why they can't take this place away from me. When I go home there's nothing.

**Sophie** We're all in the same boat.

**Hetty** She's got a rich son, she doesn't need to wait for no operation to save her eyes. You've always had everything except a husband who loves you. When he finished with that barmaid he was *shtupping* a milliner from Hollen Street.

*Magda gets her belongings ready to leave during the following*

**Magda** We were never really close friends, Hetty …

**Hetty** We were never friends.

**Magda** You're not the same person I knew. Senility has clearly affected your mind.

**Hetty** Senile! Who are you calling senile?

**Sophie** Magda, please don't say anything.

**Magda** You obviously don't know what you're saying.

**Hetty** I'm telling her the truth and she calls me senile — you're the one that's senile.

**Magda** This whole fiasco has gone far enough. When all the attention dies down, we will just be a group of foolish old women with nothing better to do. We can't win; they'll never give us back our *shul*.

**Sophie** We can sweat it out longer than them.

**Magda** Playing cards here every week kept me in touch with the old world — I can't explain it, my son doesn't understand … Max would have understood. I joined you because I thought we were doing the right thing.

**Sophie** Don't go, Magda.

**Magda** Max loved this place. It's a beautiful synagogue; it mustn't be destroyed. It's not just a building. Without it there will be no community any more. All our memories will be buried here. What is that modern expression? We must move on. I admire you, Sophie. I wouldn't have dreamed of doing what you have done. You have been so selfless. But we've been here almost three weeks, quarrelling and getting absolutely nowhere. Hetty, I've forgiven you already.

**Hetty** Forgiven me! She's forgiven me! I'm the one should be forgiving you — you stuck-up cow! (*She throws her cards across the room*)

**Magda** Hetty, you must be so unhappy to make up all those lies. Because they are lies, every single word.

*Magda exits through the window, carrying her valise and handbag. There is a pause*

**Sophie** I knew about the barmaid at the *Blue Post*.

**Hetty** The whole of Soho knew, and Fitzrovia.
**Sophie** Everybody except Magda.
**Hetty** Well, now she knows.
**Sophie** But I never knew about no milliner in Hollen Street.
**Hetty** I made it up.
**Sophie** Hetty!
**Hetty** I didn't want to let her off lightly. She's always showing off where she's going: her son's taking her here, taking her there, now he's taking her skiing ... She can't stop telling us how busy she is; Wednesday is her bridge club, Thursdays she does voluntary work ...
**Sophie** You've got to remember one thing: she's that much younger than us — at her age I also did more ...
**Hetty** She's not that young.
**Sophie** She told me she was sixty-eight last month.
**Hetty** The only time she'll see sixty-eight again is on a the front of a bus.

*Black-out*

<h2 style="text-align:center">SCENE 3</h2>

*The same. Late November. The following morning*

*A memorial candle has been set and the card table folded up. The hamper, flowers and basket have been removed*

*We hear an extract from an operatic aria. This fades*

*The Lights come up. Loretta is alone on stage, dressed in black. She lights the memorial candle*

*After a moment Sophie and Hetty enter. They are wearing black coats and hats*

**Hetty** She was my friend.
**Sophie** She was also my friend ... Who'd have thought Magda would be the first to go?
**Hetty** What about Magda's son? Who's going to tell him?
**Loretta** He already knows, he was at the funeral.
**Hetty** Good-looking boy. Magda says he doesn't like girls.
**Loretta** It hasn't quite sunk in. Magda was so full of life.
**Sophie** (*to Loretta*) Thank you for staying here.
**Loretta** One of us had to.
**Sophie** It was nice of you.

**Loretta**  Were there lots of people there?

**Sophie**  Magda would have loved it. It was a full house. Rabbi Bernstein always does it beautifully. I was hoping he'd be free.

**Hetty**  Lots of fellers there — you know, with other fellers. Looked odd ...

**Sophie**  Friends of Magda's son Simon. Magda would be so pleased you're back with us, Loretta. You can go to the *shiva*. They're only having one day, apparently.

**Hetty**  (*to Loretta*) I love you, darling ... I love everything about you, darling.

**Sophie**  I know Magda — she would have hated to become an old woman. If you've got to go ... At least she went quickly ... That's how I want to go ... A heart attack. Her cleaner found her. Her son told me. She was still in her evening dress. She looked lovely.

**Loretta**  She always did.

**Sophie**  They'd been to the opera. Her son said they'd had the most wonderful evening. They were laughing, making jokes. That's how he'll always remember her. She went out, as they say, on a high.

**Hetty**  There's a dog under the table.

**Sophie**  (*to Loretta*) She's getting worse ...

**Hetty**  It's been there all the time we've been eating.

**Hetty**  Who's taking the dog for a walk? Sophie, it's not your responsibility. Don't let him near the food ...

**Sophie**  She'll be all right in a minute ...

**Hetty**  Magda's late. Are we having a game?

**Loretta**  Hetty, we can't have a game. Magda's ...

**Sophie**  A game wouldn't be a bad idea. (*To Loretta*) It'll take her mind off things ... With all her *meshugas* she can still play Kaluki. It's a wonderful therapy. In a minute she'll remember about Magda and she'll get upset again.

**Loretta**  I'll get the table out. (*She pulls out the table and unfolds it during the following*) Michael said the developers will never give in.

**Sophie**  They've offered us money to get out of here. I don't want their lousy money; that's not what it's about.

**Loretta**  You should take it — they can afford it. Think of all the outings you could go on.

**Sophie**  We're not interested in outings, not at our age ... Hetty, come on, we're having a game.

**Hetty**  You can't play Kaluki with just two.

**Sophie**  She's right.

**Loretta**  I could play.

**Sophie**  Are you sure?

**Loretta**  I hope I won't let you down. I think I've got the hang of it.

**Sophie**  Of course you won't.

*They draw their chairs round the table*

Hetty, Loretta's playing with us. Loretta, you deal.

*Loretta deals the cards*

**Hetty** (*to Loretta*) I love you, darling, I love everything about you.
**Loretta** This is my first game of Kaluki.
**Sophie** All those years you've been watching, you'll be the star player.
**Hetty** Shouldn't we wait for Magda?
**Sophie** No, we can start without her.
**Hetty** If you say so, but she won't like it.
**Sophie** So how are you getting on with that fancy man of yours.
**Loretta** I'm not, I've left him.
**Sophie** That was brief.
**Loretta** The place was a pigsty. Piles of washing-up in the sink. He didn't have any clean clothes, the rubbish hadn't been emptied. After the first night he never touched me again. And he was out all-night mini-cabbing. And when he took his clothes off it's not so much he was fat, I was prepared for that but he's sweaty with bits of hair all over his body — and I think there was something else wrong with him — impetigo.
**Hetty** Ruthie, you've given me a lovely hand ... If I get Kaluki it'll serve Magda right for being late.
**Sophie** (*to Loretta*) With Magda gone it's taken the stuffing out of me. She'd no right to go first ... She had so much ... Ach ... We can't just sit here till we die ... I'm worried about her ... Enough is enough.
**Loretta** So what are you going to do?
**Sophie** We've made our point.
**Loretta** You can't stay here forever.
**Sophie** No ... Maybe Marble Arch isn't such a terrible thing.
**Loretta** Michael says they'll put on transport to pick you up and take you home.
**Hetty** (*gleefully picking up a card*) You must be a mind reader.
**Loretta** (*to Sophie*) What if she gets worse?
**Sophie** I can look after her.
**Loretta** I'll help you. Since Mummy died I feel lost if I'm not doing something on Tuesdays ... They don't need me at work.

*Hetty puts three sets of cards on the table*

**Hetty** Do you want to hear a funny story?
**Sophie** Not now, later maybe ...

**Hetty**  Do you remember that little salt beef bar in Windmill Street? Well there was this fella who used to come in as regular as clockwork for a salt beef on rye and a side order of new green. Then the owner found this fella eating a salt beef sandwich sitting in the window of the restaurant across the road. This happened every week until eventually the owner went over to the fella and says: "What's the matter? You don't eat by me any more. Have I offended you?" "It's like this," said the feller. "I had terrible toothache and I went to the dentist and he told me to eat on the other side!"

*The three women continue playing*

*Magda enters in full evening dress*

*The game continues. Hetty, Sophie and Loretta do not notice Magda, who stands behind Loretta, guiding her hand. Loretta wins the game*

*Opera music plays, superceded by the sounds of construction works*

*Magda moves away and the music swells up again. She turns and catches Loretta's eye*

*The Lights fade*

# FURNITURE AND PROPERTY LIST

## ACT I
### SCENE 1

*On stage*: CLUB ROOM
*On walls*: paintings, wall clock
Chairs
Baize card tables
Cupboards (doors open) full of games including Scrabble. In drawer: two packs of cards, cup, pad, pen, paper

KITCHEN AREA
Large old-fashioned oven
Sink
Fridge. *In it*: bottle of milk, sandwich ingredients and other food
Chairs
Kitchen units. *In them*: glasses, plates, sandwich-making utensils, cups, tray

*Off stage*: Large bag or holdall (**Sophie**)

*Personal*: **Hetty**: stick, handbag, little purse containing five p coins
**Magda**: handbag, little purse containing five p coins and ten pound note
**Sophie**: little purse containing five p coins, two pound coins

### SCENE 2

*No additional props*

### SCENE 3

*Off stage*: Books of raffle tickets (**Loretta**)

### SCENE 4

*Set*: Several cardboard packing boxes

# ACT II
## SCENE 1

*Set*:            Dust sheets
                Workmen's tools

*Re-set*:         Close cupboard doors

*Strike*:         Paintings

*Off stage*:      Holdall, carrier bag of food, large box containing: kettle, two flasks,
                tea bags, powdered milk, sugar; two large portable lanterns (**Sophie**)
                Holdall, carrier bag of food (**Hetty**)
                Fortnum and Mason hamper, hair drier, large roll of toilet paper, valise
                (**Magda**)
                Large bag containing mobile phone and torch (**Loretta**)

*Personal*:       **Sophie**: miner's lamp

## SCENE 2

*Set*:            Large hamper with big note saying "With love and support from the
                Oxford and Cambridge Club"
                Flower arrangement with note saying "All the best from the Stanmore
                and District Ladies' Guild"
                Large basket
                Radio cassette player
                Tapes
                Tablecloth on table
                Menorah with Chanukah candles
                *Jewish Chronicle* for **Hetty**
                Personal belongings of **Sophie, Hetty, Magda** and **Loretta**

*Strike*:         Dust sheets
                Workmen's tools

## SCENE 3

*Set*:            Memorial candle
                Matches for **Loretta**

*Re-set*:         Fold up card table

*Strike*:         Hamper
                Flower arrangement
                Large basket

# LIGHTING PLOT

Practical fittings required: two large portable lanterns, miner's lamp, torch
One interior with exterior backing beyond window. The same throughout

ACT I, SCENE 1

*To open*: General interior lighting with summer mid-morning setting on exterior backing

*Cue* 1    **Sophie**: " ... the rest of the sandwiches through for me?"    (Page 11)
           *Black-out*


ACT I, SCENE 2

*To open*: General interior lighting with summer mid-morning setting on exterior backing

*Cue* 2    **Hetty**: "You've twisted my arm."                    (Page 17)
           *Black-out*

ACT I, SCENE 3

*To open*: General interior lighting with summer mid-morning setting on exterior backing

*Cue* 3    **Sophie**: " ... we won't let them pull it down."       (Page 24)
           *Black-out*

ACT I, SCENE 4

*To open*: General interior lighting with late summer mid-morning setting on exterior backing

*Cue* 4    **Loretta**: " ... you've only got one life!"          (Page 28)
           *Black-out*

ACT II, SCENE 1

*To open*: Darkness

| *Cue* 5 | **Sophie** enters with miner's lamp | (Page 29) |
| | *Bring up covering spot on lamp* | |

| *Cue* 6 | **Sophie** switches on the lanterns | (Page 29) |
| | *Bring up covering spot on lanterns* | |

| *Cue* 7 | **Sophie** takes off the miner's lamp | (Page 29) |
| | *Cut spot on miner's lamp* | |

| *Cue* 8 | **Sophie** turns the lanterns off | (Page 33) |
| | *Cut cover spot on lanterns* | |

| *Cue* 9 | Banging on the door | (Page 33) |
| | *Flash beam of torchlight under the door* | |

| *Cue* 10 | **Hetty**: "'He says he knows you!'" | (Page 34) |
| | *Black-out* | |

ACT II, SCENE 2

*To open*: General interior lighting with autumn late afternoon setting on exterior backing. Covering spot on Chanukah candle

| *Cue* 11 | **Loretta** takes a few tentative steps | (Page 34) |
| | *Fade lights on club room* | |

| *Cue* 12 | **Sophie**: " ... I'm only doing boiled." | (Page 35) |
| | *Cross-fade to club room* | |

| *Cue* 13 | **Magda**: " ... three, four, cha-cha-cha ..." | (Page 36) |
| | *Cross-fade to kitchen* | |

| *Cue* 14 | **Sophie**: " ... or shall I make some coleslaw?" | (Page 36) |
| | *Cross-fade to club room* | |

| *Cue* 15 | **Loretta**: " But that's the trouble, Magda, I haven't." | (Page 45) |
| | *Cross-fade to kitchen* | |

| *Cue* 16 | **Hetty**: " ... on the front of a bus." | (Page 45) |
| | *Black-out* | |

ACT II, SCENE 3

*To open*: General interior lighting with morning setting on exterior backing

| *Cue* 17 | **Loretta** lights the memorial candle | (Page 45) |
| | *Cover spot on memorial candle* | |

| *Cue* 18 | **Magda** turns and catches **Loretta**'s eye | (Page 48) |
| | *Fade to black-out* | |

# EFFECTS PLOT

## ACT I

*No cues*

## ACT II

Lightning Source UK Ltd.
Milton Keynes UK
UKHW022024120319
338970UK00005B/214/P